LEARN TO READ WITH
planet earth
Workbook 1

LEVEL 2

Practice Sounds r,s,l blends wh, sh

P9-AOW-054

by Quinlan B. Lee

ISBN-13: 978-0-545-14825-2
ISBN-10: 0-545-14825-1

12 11 10 9 8 7 6 5 4 3 2

9 10 11 12 13 14/0

Printed in China
First printing, September 2009

95

R-Blend Match

Draw lines to match each *r-blend* to the correct ending sound to make a word. The clues will help you. The first one has been done for you.

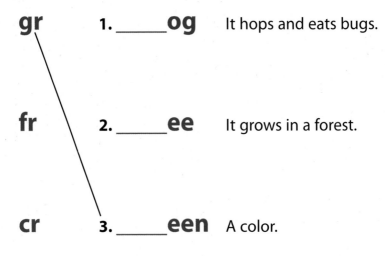

gr

1. _____**og**   It hops and eats bugs.

fr

2. _____**ee**   It grows in a forest.

cr

3. _____**een**   A color.

tr

4. _____**oak**   The sound a frog makes.

Sentence Scramble

Put the words below in the correct order to make some cool tree frog facts. Write each sentence on the lines below.

feet. frogs have Tree sticky

....

frogs in Tree live jungles.

....

drink. not frogs do Tree

....

Missing Blend

Complete each sentence by filling in an *s-blend* from the box below. The first one has been done for you.

1. Polar bears <u>st</u>ay warm.

2. Polar bears like to ___im.

3. There is a lot of ___ow in the Arctic.

4. Polar bear cubs ___eep close to their mothers.

| sl | st |
| sn | sw |

Rhyme Time

Draw a line between the polar bear word on the left to the rhyming word on the right. The first one has been done for you.

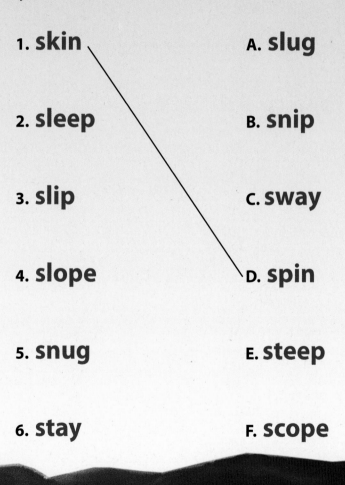

1. **skin**

2. **sleep**

3. **slip**

4. **slope**

5. **snug**

6. **stay**

A. **slug**

B. **snip**

C. **sway**

D. **spin**

E. **steep**

F. **scope**

Sentence Fill-In

Draw lines to match the polar bear facts with the correct missing word. The first one has been done for you.

1. Polar bears live in the _____.

skin

2. Polar bears have black _____ to help keep them warm.

swim

3. Polar bears can _____ fast and far in the cold water.

slide

snow

4. Polar bear cubs like to slip and _____.

Grizzly Word Search

Find these *l-blend* words in the word search. Circle each word as you find it. Look up, down, and across.

b	a	s	l	o	p	e	f
l	d	c	e	o	p	l	c
o	n	u	b	h	q	g	l
w	b	l	i	n	k	s	o
s	l	d	m	e	r	w	s
v	t	s	w	x	y	a	e
s	l	o	w	l	y	l	c
z	p	l	a	y	a	c	b

blink blows
claws close
slope slowly
play

Matching Make-a-Word

Match a beginning sound from the left with an ending from the right to make a grizzly bear word. Write the new words on the lines. The first one has been done for you.

cl	**ope**	1. _claws_
pl	**ide**	2._____
gl	**aws**	3._____
sl	**ants**	4._____

Blend Change

Change the *l-blend* in each of the words below to transform it into a new word. Use the clues to help you. The first one has been done for you.

1. **clue**   _bl_ **ue** (a color)

2. **glide**   ____**ide** (something at a playground)

3. **slack**   ____**ack** (a color)

4. **flaw**   ____**aw** (the sharp nails on a bear)

5. **bleep**   ____**eep** (the opposite of awake)

Whale of a Word Scramble

Draw lines to match the scrambled words below to the correct "wh" words.

1. rhwli   A. wham

2. mhaw   B. whine

3. lweha   C. whack

4. liehw   D. whale

5. achkw   E. whirl

6. newih   F. while

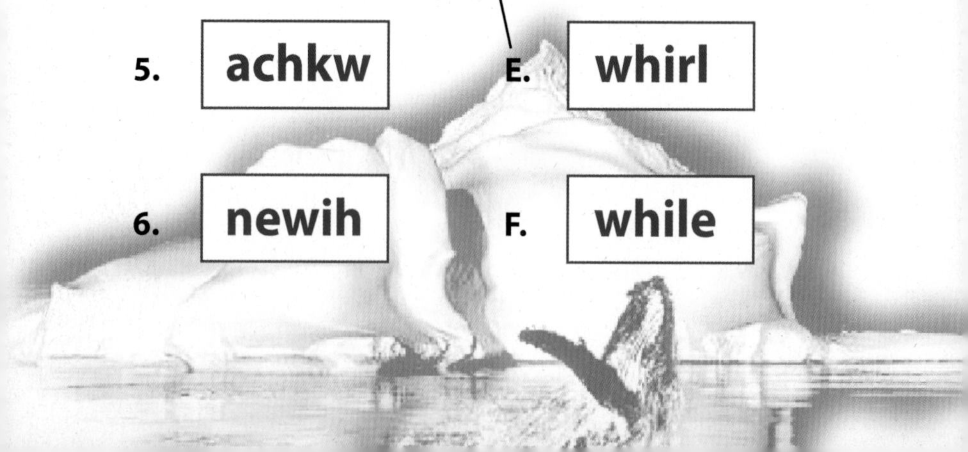

Picture Match

Put an X next to the sentence that best describes the picture on the right.

_____ **1.** Humpback whales eat small fish

_____ **2.** Whales like to whack their tails and splash.

_____ **3.** Whales whiz in a circle.

_____ **1.** Whales can whirl up out of the water.

_____ **2.** Whale songs sound like a whine.

_____ **3.** Whales open their mouths to eat fish.

Clueless Crossword

Complete the puzzle below by filling in the *wh* words
from the word box.

Z

A

W

N

L

whale

while

whine

whirl

whiz

"Sh" Words

Write the letters "sh" on the lines below to complete the words. Then choose the two words that best complete the sentences and write them on the lines.

swi_____

_____ape

fi_____

_____arp

Sharks are _____.

Sharks _____ through the water.

Sentence Fill-In

Choose a word from the box that best completes each sentence. Then write the word on the blank.

fresh	**sharks**	**sharp**	**shed**

1. Some _____ live in _____ water.

2. Most sharks' teeth are _____.

3. Sharks _____ teeth all the time.

Sentence Scramble

Unscramble these sentences to learn more fun facts about sharks. Write each sentence on the line below.

are sharks big. Some

....

stop Sharks swimming. never

....

lots have teeth. Sharks of

....

Answer Page

Page 2
1. frog, 2. tree, 3. green, 4. croak

Page 3
Tree frogs have sticky feet.

Tree frogs live in jungles.

Tree frogs do not drink.

Page 4
1. stay, 2. swim, 3. snow, 4. sleep

Page 5
1. - D, 2. - E, 3. - B, 4. - F, 5. - A, 6. - C

Page 6
1. snow, 2. skin, 3. swim, 4. slide

Page 7

Page 8
1. claws, 2. plants, 3. glide, 4. slope

Page 9
1. blue, 2. slide, 3. black,
4. claw, 5. sleep

Page 10
1. - E, 2. - A, 3. - D,
4. - F, 5. - C, 6. - B

Page 11
2. Whales like to whack
   their tails and splash.

1. Whales can whirl up out
   of the water.

Page 12

Page 13
swish, shape, fish, sharp
Sharks are fish.
Sharks swish through the water.

Page 14
1. sharks/fresh 2. sharp 3. shed

Page 15
Some sharks are big.
Sharks never stop swimming.
Sharks have lots of teeth.